A BEGINNER'S GUIDE TO SIMPLE DRESSMAKING

- WITH INSTRUCTIONS ON HOW TO MAKE A SIMPLE COAT -

BY

SARAH G. SERVICE

Copyright © 2011 Read Books Ltd.
This book is copyright and may not be
reproduced or copied in any way without
the express permission of the publisher in writing

British Library Cataloguing-in-Publication Data
A catalogue record for this book is available from
the British Library

CONTENTS

Equipment, Materials, Cutting Out, etc.

General Hints and Methods

Making a Simple Coat

SIMPLE DRESSMAKING

SARAH G. SERVICE

EVERY woman at some time in her life has the ambition to make a dress, skirt or blouse. Few can withstand the creative impulse to see something being assembled bit by bit under their own hands. Some, for lack of time, do not carry out this desire, but those who have can make it a very profitable and enjoyable hobby.

Gone are the days of laboured work in dressmaking. Our grandmothers and great-grandmothers were arrayed in the most wonderful creations, frills upon frills, buttonholes and buttons by the score, seams and more seams. Indeed the time and labour spent on one frock of those days would produce twelve very stylish modes of to-day.

Then at this moment we have materials and colours which are a perfect joy to handle and so inexpensive. Also one can buy patterns which make the creation of smart dresses simplicity itself. The cut is so good, the directions so clearly given, and the difficulties of making-up are reduced to a minimum.

The success of home-made garments is largely due to the choice of materials, a reliable pattern, simplicity of style, a good set of sewing tools and careful preparation of every step in the making up. If the following simple directions are strictly adhered to there should be no difficulty in producing a well-finished garment.

EQUIPMENT. A large unpolished surface for cutting-out purposes. If you have not a good-sized table the floor is a very good substitute.

2. A pair of large cutting-out scissors.
3. A pair of small scissors with sharp points for cutting buttonholes.
4. Small steel pins and Lille pins for fine materials. Pin tray.
5. Various sizes of needles.
6. Tacking thread, white and coloured.
7. Sewing thread, black and white cotton.
8. Yard stick and inch tape.
9. Tailor's chalk.
10. Thimble, one which fits well and not too rough on the outside.
11. Pressing roller.
12. Iron, ironing blanket and sheet, ironing board.

SIMPLE DRESSMAKING

13. Damping cloth, which should be of cotton and free from dressing.

To Calculate the Quantity of Material Required. For garments cut on the cross or having flares or pleats more material may be required, but with most good paper patterns a table of the necessary quantities is supplied.

Garment	Estimated Length of Material Required	Width of Material	Example of Quantity Required
Blouse	Twice length of blouse + length of sleeve.	38"	Blouse=22". Sleeve =22" ∴ 2×22"=44" +22" = 2 yds.
Dress	Twice length of dress from shoulder to hem +4" for hem and once length of sleeve.	38"	Dress=45"+4". Sleeve=22" ∴ 2×49" = 98" + 22" = 120" =3⅓ yds.
,,	Twice length of garment + 4" hem.	54"	Dress = 45" + 4" ∴ 2 × 49"=98"= 2¾ yds.
Skirt	Twice length of skirt + 4" hem.	38"	Skirt = 32" + 4" ∴ 2 × 36" = 2 yds.
,,	1½ times length of skirt + 4" hem.	54"	Skirt = 32" + 4" ∴ 1½ × 36 = 1½ yds.
Jacket	Twice length of jacket + 2" hem and length of sleeve.	38"	Jacket = 23" + 2" Sleeve = 22" ∴ 2 × 25" = 50" + 22" = 2 yds.
,,	Once length of jacket + 2" hem and length of sleeve.	54"	Jacket = 23" + 2" Sleeve = 22" = 25" + 22" = 1¼ yds.

MATERIALS. The cut and line of garments change each year, and side by side march the advancement of colour and materials. Materials may be grouped under linens, cotton, wool, silk and artificial silk, but there are many names given to materials classed under each group, according to the weave or chemical treatment which the fabric undergoes during the process of manufacture. Each season produces something new and attractive. Such is the progress of textiles, and it must be admitted that the materials of to-day are much more distinctive than those of yesterday. They may not be so durable, or be expected to last for years, but then we of this generation must have many changes, and above all we must be gay.

Here are a few names which may guide you when choosing materials for the garment you purpose making.

SIMPLE DRESSMAKING

Material	Width	Description	Use
Linen.	36"-54"	Twilled or plain weave, heavy quality.	Cruising wear.
	36"-54"	Plain weave, fine quality.	Overalls and frocks.
Cottons.			
Zephyr and Gingham	38"	Plain weave pattern same on both sides.	Overalls and Summer frocks.
Tobralco	38"	Firm hair cord surface, printed on right side.	Tennis frocks and children's wear.
Piqué	38"	Firm-corded surface, self-colours only.	Tennis frocks, collars and cuffs.
Voile	38"	Plain weave and transparent.	Summer frocks.
Organdie	38"	Crisp and transparent.	Summer frocks.
Velveteen	24"-40"	Thick all-cotton pile.	Winter frocks and wraps.
Silks.			
Crêpe-de-chine	38"	Very fine shiny crinkled surface.	Blouses and frocks.
Marocain	38"	Very fine cord and slightly crinkled.	Afternoon frocks.
Poplin	38"	Fine cord and smooth surface.	Afternoon frocks.
Taffeta	38"	Crisp and plain smooth surface.	Evening frocks.
Satin Charmeuse	38"	Very glossy surface and dull on wrong side.	Blouses and Evening frocks.
Ninon	38"	Thin gauze with shiny surface.	Evening frocks.
Georgette	38"	Thin gauze with a crinkled surface.	Evening frocks.
Velvet	18"-36"	All silk piled material, very light weight.	Evening frocks and wraps.
Artificial Silks.	38"	May be a mixture of silk and cotton, or may be prepared from wood or cotton by treatment with chemicals.	Day or Evening frocks.
Woollens.			
Tweed	54"	Heavy rough surface.	For country and sports wear.

SIMPLE DRESSMAKING

Material	Width	Description	Use
Serge	54"	Twilled smooth surface.	For country and sports wear.
Marocain	54"	Fine crinkled surface.	Dresses and Costumes.
Repp	54"	Fine cord running from selvedge to selvedge.	,, ,, ,,
Hopsack	54"	A plain weave closely woven.	,, ,, ,,
Angora	54"	A soft, silky material with a twill weave.	Dresses.
Mixtures.		Found in the cheaper makes of material, and may be a mixture of wool and cotton, silk and cotton, or linen and cotton.	

PLACING AND CUTTING OUT. Do not cut out in a hurry. If your time is limited, then leave it to another day.

All parts of garments should have the strong thread running lengthwise (i.e. selvedge way), neck to waist, waist to hem. Armhole to wrist of sleeve, etc. Collars and cuffs, if straight, have the strong thread running lengthwise. Sleeves must have the straight thread running from shoulder to wrist on a full sleeve and from shoulder to elbow on a shaped sleeve.

Place the largest and widest part of the pattern to the cut edge of the material. Dovetail the pieces of pattern when possible. This, of course, cannot be done on non-reversible materials, such as velvets or a one-way patterned fabric. Place all pieces of pattern on to the material before cutting out, noticing which edges of the pattern must be placed to a fold of material.

All stripes must match at seams. If the material has a broad stripe place the centre front and centre back of pattern to the middle of the stripe. All floral designs should have the pattern growing upwards on all parts of the garment. Checks must be matched at the seams, both across and lengthwise.

If the material has no decided right and wrong side, always pin-mark the right sides of each piece before separating. This prevents any mistake when making up.

Pin the pattern carefully at each corner and along the sides.

Cut with good even strokes, leaving turnings as directed in the instructions.

Hold material firmly down with the left hand.

Keep all corners sharp.

Order of Making Up Simple Garments

Jumper Blouse.
   1. Cut out. Make special markings for darts, joining places, etc.
   2. Tack up and fit.
   3. Join shoulder seams, side seams and sleeve seams.
   4. Finish bottom edge. Finish fronts or make neck opening.
   5. Finish neck line with collar or binding.
   6. Make opening on sleeve and set on cuff.
   7. Set in sleeves.
   8. Press carefully.
   9. Sew on fasteners, or make buttonholes and sew on buttons.

Skirt.
   1. Cut out. Tailor-tack position of pockets, darts, etc, if any. Mark centre front.
   2. Tack up and fit.
   3. Machine-stitch darts and seams all but placket opening.
   4. Press seams.
   5. Make placket, and pockets, if any.
   6. Finish raw edges of seams.
   7. Mount to waist banding.
   8. Turn up bottom hem and bind.
   9. Give final press. Sew on fasteners.

Dress.
   1. Cut out. Mark centre front. Tailor tack position of pockets, if any.
   2. Arrange pleats, godets, or flares to skirt part, if any.
   3. Tack top of front to skirt front.
   4. Tack top and back to skirt back. If backs and fronts are in one piece, then 3 and 4 are not necessary.
   5. Tack the side seams and sleeve seams, then fit.
   6. Unpick side seams and machine-stitch the top and skirt of front together. Do likewise with the back pieces.
   7. Machine-stitch the side seams. This is a much quicker and easier method than making up the top and the skirt separately, then joining together.
   8. Finish the raw edges of seams.
   9. Make opening if necessary at neck or waist.
   10. Make pockets, if any.
   11. Make collar and fix to neck or finish neck as desired.
   12. Make sleeves, then set in. Finish sleeve seams.
   13. Make belt.
   14. Give final press.
   15. Sew on fasteners, buttons, etc.

SIMPLE DRESSMAKING

Things Worth Knowing

Always pin a hem or seam before tacking.
Always thread needle as thread comes off bobbin. This prevents the thread from twisting or forming knots.

Never use a long thread, except when basting.

Tack each hem or seam before sewing and machine-stitching. This may seem extra labour, but it saves time in the long run.

Use suitable thread-silk thread for silk or fine woollen materials, cotton thread for cotton or linen, mercerised thread for artificial silk or woollen material.

Be careful to choose a good match of thread and a shade darker than the fabric, because the single thread always works up lighter than it appears on the spool or bobbin.

If the hands perspire, the moisture makes the needle and thread sticky. It gives the work a soiled appearance and makes the worker uncomfortable. To prevent this rub the hands with talcum powder or carbonate of magnesia.

Always machine-stitch seams from the top downwards, e.g. from the waist to the hem of a skirt.

Always machine-stitch circular parts, such as armholes, wrists, etc., from the inside, so that the curves may be maintained while the machining is being done.

When stitching a gathered part always keep the gathered side up.

When stitching thin materials liable to stretch out of shape or pucker up, tack a piece of tissue or similar paper underneath and tear away after stitching.

Materials with a pile, such as velvet and velour, should be stitched *with* the pile to prevent the pressure foot marking the fabric.

Always snick the seam right to the machine-stitching on an inward curve and snip V-shaped pieces out of the seam of an outward curve when these have to be turned to the inside.

Always stretch binding to an inward curve, such as the neck and armholes.

Always ease binding to an outward curve, such as the outer curve of a collar.

Never have pins left in a seam which you are going to machine-stitch. There is always the danger of the pin going through with the seam, and if so the machine needle will certainly break.

Never stitch through a tacking thread knot. This is apt to make the needle stick and the thread in the machine will break.

When joining machine-stitching, pull the broken ends through to the wrong side, if there is no hem. If there is a hem, pull the

SIMPLE DRESSMAKING

upper and under threads between the fold just as in hemming, and tuck both underneath. Start anew four stitches back and machine-stitch over these. Pull the upper thread through to the wrong side and tie, or thread on to a needle and make a small stitch. A join made like this is almost invisible.

Never have more than ¼ inch lay on the turning of a hem on cotton or thin materials, and never more than ½-inch on woollen or thick materials.

Iron or press down the lay of a hem wherever possible. This makes it easier to prepare the hem and makes a neater job.

STITCHES

TACKING. A temporary stitch used to hold hems and seams in position until machined or hand-sewn.

Work from right towards left. Lift ¼-inch on to needle and pass over about ½-inch. (*Fig. 1.*)

BASTING. A temporary stitch used to hold lining and material together, or to fix a band to gathers or pleats. Work from right towards left. Insert needle perpendicularly, lifting ½ inch on to

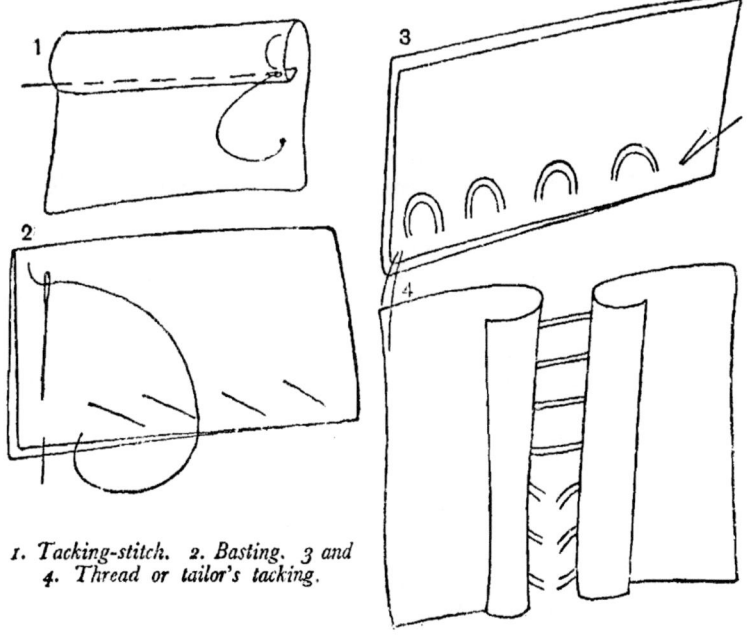

1. Tacking-stitch. 2. Basting. 3 and 4. Thread or tailor's tacking.

needle. Pass over ½-inch to 1½ inches, according to part being basted. *Note* the thread forms a sloping stitch. (*Fig. 2.*)

A temporary stitch used to mark, fitting lines, position of darts, pockets, curves, etc., on two pieces of material at the same time (e.g. two corresponding parts of a skirt, two sleeves, etc.).

TAILOR'S TACKING. Place right sides together. Use a long, double tacking thread. Lift ½-inch to ¾-inch, pass over ½-inch to ¾-inch and leave a loop of thread standing up. (*Fig. 3.*)

Follow the required line. Draw the two pieces of material apart as far as the loop will allow. Cut the strands of thread across in the middle, as shown in *Fig. 4*. This leaves a mark on right side of both pieces of material.

FITTING

HAVE centre-front, centre-back and waist-line clearly marked. Tack pieces of garment together firmly, taking care to have the beginning and end of tacking thread securely fastened, lest the seams become undone when the garment is put on the wearer. The garment should be fitted with the right side out, otherwise the garment may not fit properly when finished. Fit the right-hand side from the front, and the left-hand side from the back, inserting the pins downwards.

WHERE TO FIT DRESS. Shoulder seams, side seams, waist-line, armhole curves and length are where the points of alteration are made. Unpick all seams where fitting is required, as the alteration sometimes requires to be taken off one side only.

Note length first, and make alterations if necessary at the shoulder seams. Should a garment poke in front at waist or bottom hem, let the front shoulder down at the neck point and lift slightly at the armhole. Take in or let out garments at the side seams.

A close fit is required round the neck and armholes, flat across the shoulders, with ease at the bust line. Chalk or pin mark the correct line at the neck, armhole and waist. The length of garment is usually regulated from the ground up, using a yard stick and chalk to mark the length required. When this is being done it is of great advantage to the fitter to have the person being fitted standing on a raised platform, e.g. a table. A better line is obtained and the fitting is got over much quicker.

FITTING SLEEVES. Have a gathering thread run round the top of the sleeve about ½-inch from the edge. Put the sleeve on and pin the top of the sleeve to the fitting line, taking care to have the straight thread of sleeve running in a line with the top of the armhole, a point immediately opposite the under-arm seam, and not the shoulder seam. This will ensure a good hang to the sleeve, and should not drag or twist. Mark the position of the

SIMPLE DRESSMAKING

sleeve seam, which may not fall in a line with the under-arm seam of the blouse or dress, but in all probability about 1 inch in front of the seam.

If the sleeve is a fitting one, bend the arm, see that there is sufficient room for movement, and mark the elbow point. Correct the line at the wrist.

FITTING SKIRTS. When fitting a skirt it is wise to have the waist-band prepared with hooks and eyes to fit the waist. Mark the centre-front and centre-back of band, as it will be when worn. Usually a skirt fastens at the left-hand side, so that the centre-front of band will be marked about 4 inches to 6 inches from hook side. Fasten hooks and eyes, fold down by centre-front mark, and centre-back will be found. Pin centre-front and centre-back of skirt to centre front and centre back of band, pin side points, then arrange the rest at regular intervals.

The seams of a skirt should fall straight from the waist to the bottom hem. Get the waist fitting neatly, then should any seam twist towards the back, unpick that seam and let the back edge fall over the front to take a straight line, then pin into position. If the skirt is gathered at the waist, arrange the gathers to lie straight. If darted at the waist, the darts must run straight from the waist towards the hip and must taper out to a thread. Darts must not go beyond the hip line. Level the bottom edge of the skirt from the ground up.

When the garment has been fitted, trace out all fitting lines with tacking thread before removing the pins.

SEAMS USED IN DRESSMAKING

OPEN SEAM. Used on woollen materials, and is the simplest seam of all to make.

Place right sides together with edges meeting. Tack and machine-stitch by fitting line. Press flat and finish raw edges by overcasting, or binding with Paris binding or silk-bias binding.

A=overcast edge. B=bound edge. (*Fig. 5.*)

RAISED SEAM. Used on woollen materials, and is a more decorative method than the plain seam. (*Fig. 6 and 7.*)

Place right sides together, with edges meeting and tack on the wrong side by fitting line. Lay both turnings to one side and tack down on the right side. Machine-stitch from right side ¼-inch from fold. Both turnings are finished together with binding.

SLOT SEAM. This seam appears like two tucks touching each other. Place right sides together and tack on the wrong side by fitting line, and press open. Cut a strip of material selvedge way the length required and 1½ inches to 2 inches wider than the desired

SIMPLE DRESSMAKING

width of seam. Place centre of strip to the seam on wrong side of the garment and tack down. On the right side machine-stitch down each side ½ inch or less from the edges tacked together. (*Fig. 8*).

FINISHING RAW EDGES OF SEAMS. Use Paris binding for heavy woollen materials. Silk-bias binding for fine woollen materials. Fold ⅓ of binding over and press firmly. Sometimes this is ironed down to keep it flat. (*Fig. 9.*) Slip the raw edge of seam between the edges of binding, keeping the narrow edge uppermost. Tack and machine-stitch on right side exactly on the edge. (*Fig. 10.*) One row of machine-stitching is sufficient to hold both edges of the binding because of the under edge being wider than the top edge.

Bias binding is applied in the same way.

BLANKET STITCH. Used on all kinds of woollen materials. (*Fig. 11.*) Hold the edge downwards and work from left towards right. Full directions given for this stitch in needlework section.

5. *Open seam.*—A overcast edge; B bound edge.
6 and 7. *Raised seam.* 8. *Slot seam.*—*Strip of material laid to wrong side of seam.*

OVERCASTING. Used on closely-woven woollen materials. (*Fig. 12.*)

NOTCHED OR PINKED. Cut into regular V-shapes with sharp scissors along the cut edge used on very thick or closely-woven materials. Never used on materials which fray. (*Fig. 13.*)

EDGES TURNED IN. Only suitable for fine woollen, silk, cotton, or linen fabrics. Fold back the single edge of each turning to wrong side of material. Run stitch by hand if the material is inclined to fray. Machine stitch if material is closely-woven and not too fine. (*Fig. 14.*)

SIMPLE DRESSMAKING

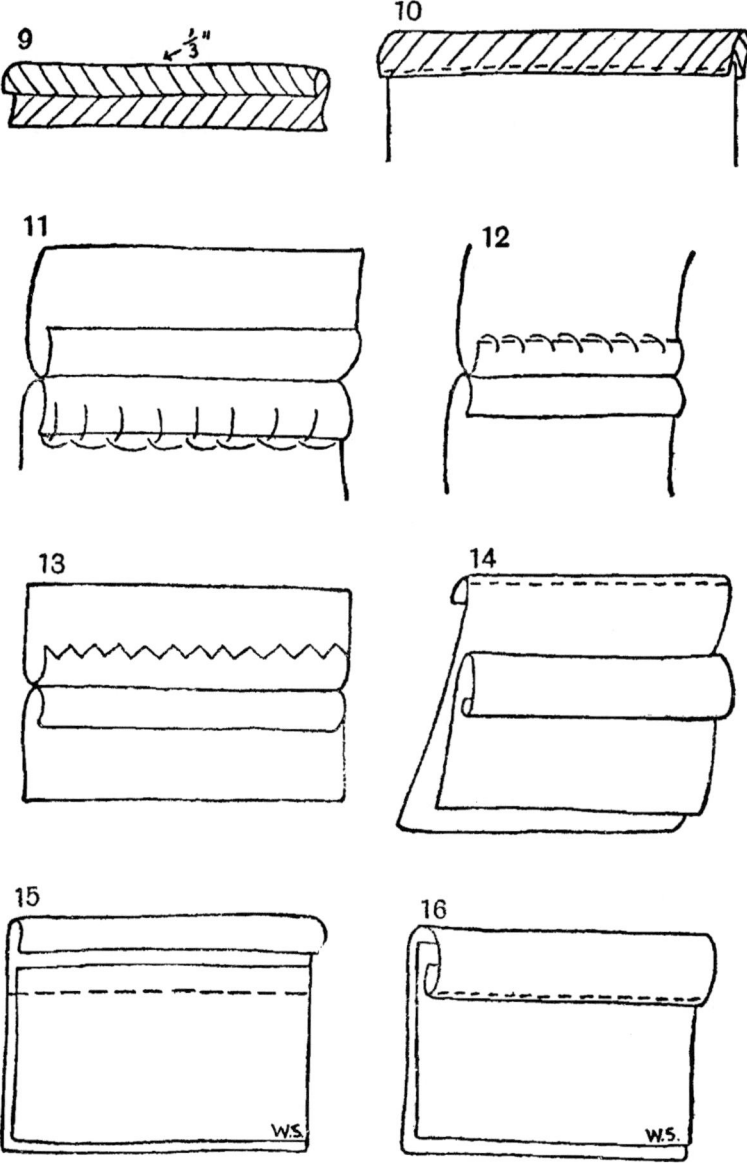

Finishing raw edges of seams. 9. Binding folded over $\frac{1}{3}$-inch. 10. Binding machined to edge of seam. 11. Blanket-stitch. 12. Overcasting. 13. Notched or pinked. 14. Edges turned in. 15 and 16. Mantua Maker's seam.

SIMPLE DRESSMAKING

Seams Suitable for Washing Materials.

FRENCH SEAM. Used for silk, cotton, linen or artificial silk. For directions see needlework section.

PLAIN SEAM. Used for silk, piqué, linen or artificial silk. Finish raw edges by turning in an edge and running or machine-stitching.

MANTUA MAKER'S SEAM. A quickly-made seam and is suitable for overalls or under-skirts made of cotton.

Tack the seam down by the fitting line with right sides together. Cut a turning from one edge, leaving the other long enough to turn down to touch the edge just cut. Fold over to make a hem along the original tacking line and machine-stitch down. The neatening and the seam are finished with one row of stitching. (*Figs. 15 and 16.*)

Pressing

THE iron plays a very important part in the making of a garment, and cannot be over-emphasised. It may make or mar a garment, and it is here that the amateur generally fails. Too much pressing is just as liable to spoil the look of a garment as an insufficient use of the iron.

1. Remove all tacking threads from seams and hems before pressing.
2. Press on the wrong side; but sometimes pressure is required on the right side, and in this case place a cloth over the part to be pressed.
3. Press each part of the work as it is completed.
4. Do not rub as in laundry work. Lift the iron and press firmly, but on no account allow the iron to remain on the one part for more than a few seconds.
5. The finished edges of seams should be pressed first, then the seam itself should be pressed over a roller. This gives a nice flat appearance.
6. Woollen materials require to be damped before pressing to give the necessary smoothness, but never damp silk fabrics.
7. To damp seams dip the tips of the fingers in water and draw them along the seam.
8. Darts should be slit open and pressed from the top down, using the point of the iron at the tapered end.
9. Where fulness has to be disposed, damp a piece of soft cotton material, place it over the fulness and with a hot iron shrink until the necessary effect is obtained.
10. Embroidery and lace should be pressed on the wrong side over a very thick padded surface.

SIMPLE DRESSMAKING

11. Velvet and pile fabrics should not be pressed over a flat surface, but should be done over an upturned iron. Another method to press velvet seams is to hold the part to be pressed between two people and then run the iron along the suspended seam.

Never press on the top of gathers, but run the point of the iron up to meet the gathered edges.

PRESSING SLEEVES. Press round the top of sleeve by making a pad of material large enough to fit into the top of the armhole. Hold this into position with the left hand. Place a damp cloth over the right side of top of sleeve and press quickly. This gives a nice flat appearance to the top of sleeve.

PRESSING PLEATS. Press very firmly so as to have each pleat sharply defined with a knife-like edge. Place the pleated material flat on to an ironing table, with wrong side uppermost. Soak a piece of cotton in water, wring it out tightly and place it over the pleats. To prevent stretching the pleats, do not rub the iron up and down, but lift and lay the iron across the pleats with a firm steady pressure. Turn to right side of pleats and repeat the process, soaking and wringing the cloth again if necessary. Remove tacking threads without disarranging the pleats, then place a damp cloth over them and press lightly. This will remove the unsightly marks of tacking threads. Should the garment have many pleats, as in a kilted skirt, the removing of the tacking threads is done three or four pleats at a time, otherwise the pleats will get hopelessly out of control. Baste each pleat into position at the bottom edge and half-way up if pleats are long. These are not removed until the garment is finished. The pressing of pleats is somewhat lengthy, but when carefully done ensures a permanent edge and flat, hanging position.

PRESSING OFF WOOLLEN GARMENTS. When a garment is finished the whole piece of work requires a final press in order to raise the surface of the material, and take away the handled look. Soak a piece of soft cotton or butter muslin in water, wring it out and place it over the right side of the garment. With a hot iron press lightly over the cloth in such a way as to allow the steam to act on the material without putting any pressure on the surface. If pressure is used then the mark of the iron will be left on the material, and this must be avoided.

COTTON AND LINEN GARMENTS. Soak a piece of cotton in water, wring it out tightly, and with it rub the surface of wrong side of garment and iron till dry. Instead of damping the surface of garment, place the damp cloth over wrong side and iron till dry. Both methods are good.

SILK GARMENTS. Do not damp silk fabrics, merely iron on the wrong side.

Methods of Disposing Fulness

GATHERS. This method is used on light-weight materials, such as silk, cotton, linen, artificial silk and very fine woollen fabrics. The amount required for gathering is $1\frac{1}{2}$ times the desired width when finished. Before gathering up a length, e.g., a skirt into a bodice, mark the centre-front, centre-back, and quarter points on both shirt and bodice, so that when joining together these points meet, and the gathers are evenly regulated. Gathers on dress materials cannot be stroked, so in order to make them set nicely two or more rows of gathers are made $\frac{1}{4}$-inch to $\frac{1}{2}$-inch apart.

TUCKS. A tuck is a fold of material held firmly in position by means of running stitches or machine-stitching. Tucks may be used as a decoration only, to dispose of fulness, or to reduce in length. When used as a decoration they are as a rule very tiny, lifting from $\frac{1}{16}$-inch to $\frac{1}{4}$-inch, and are called " pin tucks." The amount of material required for tucking is three times its width ; the under part, the upper part, and the part it lies on, e.g., three 1-inch tucks to fit into a 3-inch band requires 9 inches. Should a space of 1 inch be desired between each tuck then only twice the amount is required.

A very good and easy method of preparing tucks is first to make a tuck marker out of cardboard or stiff paper, Cut notches to give the width of tuck and the size of the space between it and the next. If there is a space between the tucks, then the tuck marker should be notched to give the depth of tuck, the under part of tuck, and the space between.

PLEATS. A pleat is a fold of material used to dispose of fulness in a decorative manner. These may be used on all kinds of material. The preparation of pleats is similar to that of tucks. The only difference being that pleats are never stitched all the way down. They usually hang free from the top fixture, but sometimes they are machine-stitched on the edge, part of the way, falling free at the bottom edge.

KNIFE PLEATS. This method has the pleats arranged so that the top edge of one pleat meets the under edge of the next pleat. The amount of material required is three times the finished width.

BOX PLEATS. These pleats have the appearance of a pleat facing towards the right and one towards the left. The amount of material required is three times the finished width.

The quickest method of working these pleats is to tack a pleat twice the width required. Crease-mark, chalk-mark, or thread-mark the edge of pleat then flatten down so that the marking is now in the centre lying on top of the tacking.

SIMPLE DRESSMAKING

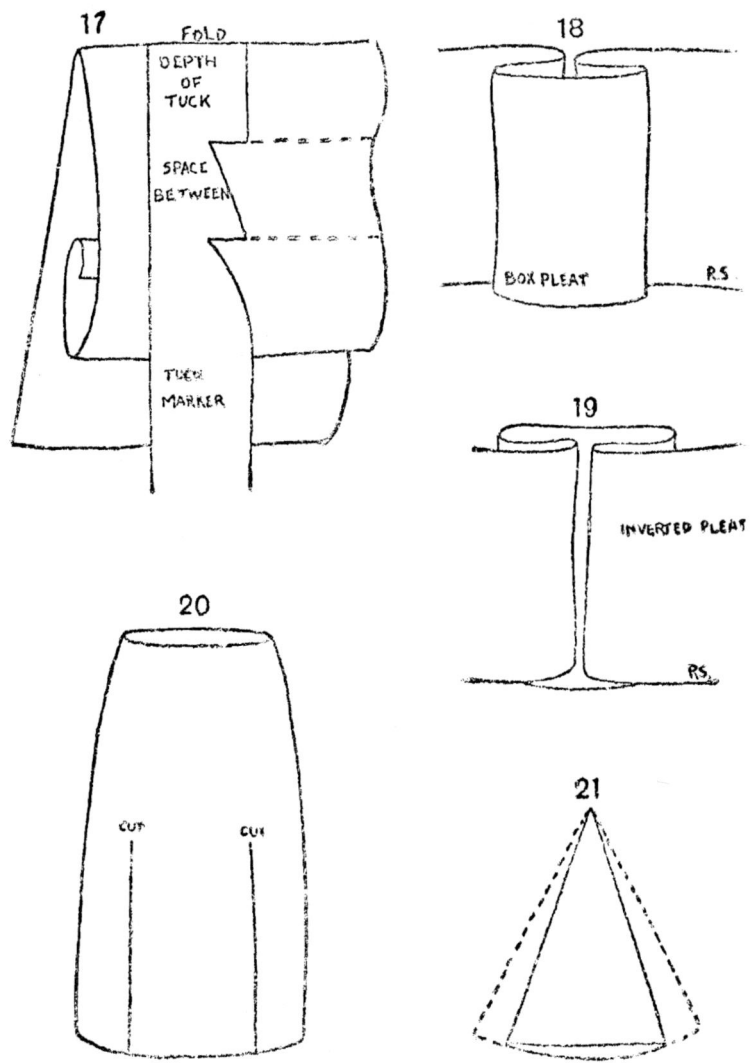

Methods of disposing fulness.—17. *Showing the use of tuck marker preparing a tuck at foot of skirt.* 18. *Box-pleat.* 19. *Inverted pleat.* 20. *Foundation skirt showing the position and length of godets.* 21. *Shape of godet, which may be anything from 6 to 24 inches at the bottom edge, tapering to a point at the top.*

INVERTED PLEATS. This method of pleating is the reverse of box pleating. Proceed as directed above, but instead of tacking a pleat to the right side and flattening, tack a pleat to the wrong side and flatten.

DARTS. Darts are used to dispose of fulness and to give a flat appearance to the garment. These may be arranged as follows :—
1. From the shoulder tapering to the bust-line.
2. From the waist upwards, tapering towards the bust-line.
3. From the waist downwards, tapering towards the hip-line.
4. From the wrist, tapering towards the elbow.
5. Sometimes small darts are taken at the front under-arm seam in order to give sufficient ease across the bust and yet give a neat, plain appearance.
6. Darts are sometimes taken at the neck and these must always radiate from the neck curve.
7. If a dart is taken at the waist of a frock, tapering upwards and downwards, it is cut across the middle right into the machine-stitching, then cut open ready for pressing. This is necessary in order to prevent a puckered appearance.
8. Darts must not go beyond the hip, bust, or elbow, and must taper to a thread. If this is not observed an ugly pleat will appear on the right side, which no amount of moisture or pressure will shrink away.

HOW TO LIFT A DART. The darts are thread-marked, or chalk-marked on to the material before the pattern is removed. Find the centre of the dart, then fold from this point down to the end of the dart. Pin from the fold out the amount to be lifted, and graduate towards the end of dart. Tack by the pins and you now have a piece of material tacked in a wedge-shape. Fit, and alter if necessary. Machine-stitch by the tacking thread beginning at the wide end and tapering out to the point.

FRILLS, FLOUNCES, FLARES, AND GODETS

FRILLS. These are used on skirts and sleeves to give a full, fluffy effect. They may be cut straight, cross, or shaped. Narrow frills are better cut on the straight or cross. If straight they should be cut across from selvedge to selvedge of the material. Frills must hang gracefully and if cut the wrong way of the material they will poke out and have a stiff appearance. For a straight frill allow $1\frac{1}{2}$ to 2 times the finished size.

The bottom edge of frills may be finished with a very narrow stitched hem, or picot edged. The joins in frills should be made with a single seam.

APPLICATION OF FRILLS.

First Method. Mark the half and quarter points along the top

SIMPLE DRESSMAKING

of the frill and the line on the skirt to which the frill is to be attached. Gather the frill, each quarter separately. Place the quarter points of frill and skirt together with the frill upside down and right sides touching. Machine-stitch by the gathering thread. Turn the frill down into position and the raw edges are hidden.

Second Method. Prepare as for first method. Make a narrow turning along top edge of frill and gather each quarter separately. Place corresponding points of frill and skirt together. In this way the fulness of frill is evenly arranged. Tack and back-stitch to skirt by the gathering thread.

Little pleated frills make a delightful trimming and look best when about 1 inch to 1½ inches wide. First cut strips of material perfectly straight the depth required and 3 to 3½ times the finished size. Make and machine-stitch a very narrow hem along the bottom edge. You will save hours of labour if you take this prepared material to the haberdashery department of any large warehouse. They will pleat it up for you for a very small charge and in a very short time.

FLOUNCES. These are similar to frills only much deeper. They may be cut straight, cross, or shaped. Prepare and finish bottom edge as for narrow frills.

Shaped flounces are very graceful and look best when made of voile, ninon, gorgette, or crêpe-de-chine. These fit without any fulness at the top edge, and are full and very frilly at the bottom edge. Flounces are mounted on to a foundation skirt and there may be two to six or even more, one above the other as the fashion decrees. To apply a shaped flounce to a skirt make a narrow turning along the top edge of flounce, then tack to skirt and machine stitch by the edge.

FLARES. These are shaped skirts similar to shaped flounces, but they are not mounted on to a foundation skirt, they hang from a hip yoke or from just above the knee line. Apply to yoke by making a ½-inch turning on the bottom edge of yoke and placing it over the top edge of flare. Machine-stitch by the edge. Finish the bottom edge of flare with a narrow stitched hem, picot-edging or bind with cross-cut pieces.

GODETS. These are shaped inlets and are to be found at regular intervals round the foot of skirts and sleeves. These are used when a plain fitting appearance is required and the fulness to spring from the knee or elbow.

Setting-in Godets to a Skirt. The foundation skirt is perfectly straight, fitting plain over the hips. Mark at the bottom edge, at regular intervals the position of godets. Cut from these points straight up by a thread, stopping just below the hip line on length of godet. Make a turning on both edges of the cut then tack to the edge of godet. By doing this you have the straight edge

SIMPLE DRESSMAKING

against the bias edge of the godet which makes a much neater seam. Machine-stitch just by the edge, taking care to make the turning at the top of godet perfectly neat. Finish the bottom edge with a $\frac{1}{8}$-inch stitched hem, picot-edging, or bind it with cross-cut pieces.

METHODS OF FINISHING SKIRT HEMS

SLIP HEM. Suitable for fine woollen, cotton, silk, and artificial silk fabrics.

Turn up to wrong side the bottom edge by fitting line, and tack. Level the turning to the desired width. Make $\frac{1}{4}$-inch lay, tack down to skirt and slip hem.

Slip hemming is worked by picking up a very small stitch of the material, then slip the needle along the edge of the fold of hem. There should be no sign of stitches showing through to the right side of material.

FRENCH HEM. Suitable for fine cotton, silk, and artificial silk fabrics. This method lends itself to circular skirts, and resembles a binding when finished.

Turn up to right side bottom edge by fitting line. Machine-stitch $\frac{1}{4}$-inch or less from the fold. Trim the turning to $\frac{3}{4}$-inch, turn it over the edge to wrong side and hem just touching the machine-stitching.

BINDING. Suitable for cotton, silk and artificial silk fabrics.

Use cross-cut strips—see directions for Cross-Cuts and Their Uses. Cut edge of skirt by fitting line. Place right side of cross strip to right side of garment with edges meeting. Machine-stitch or run and back-stitch $\frac{1}{4}$-inch or less from the edge. Be very careful not to stretch the garment when you sew on the binding. Trim edges, turn cross-strip over the edge on to wrong side and hem just above the first row of sewing. Care must be taken to have the binding firm at the edge. Stitches must not show through to right side. If the material is very fine the cross-strips may be put on double. This gives extra strength and firmness.

FLAT BINDING. Suitable for tweed, or heavy fabrics. Use Paris binding or silk bias binding for finer materials.

Turn to the wrong side the bottom edge of skirt by the fitting line. Trim the turning to make the same width all round. Place and tack the binding flat on to the edge of the turning and machine-stitch along the edge of binding. Slip hem the top edge of binding to the skirt. This makes a very flat hem.

PICOT FINISH. This is a very quick method suitable for silk or artificial silk.

Mark the bottom edge by the fitting line and picot edge. You

SIMPLE DRESSMAKING

can have this done for little cost at any of the dressmaking establishments.

Should a stronger finish be required turn the picot edge up ⅛-inch and machine-stitch by the edge.

MITRING A CORNER. Measure along both sides from the corner twice the depth of hem required plus ¼-inch for a turning.

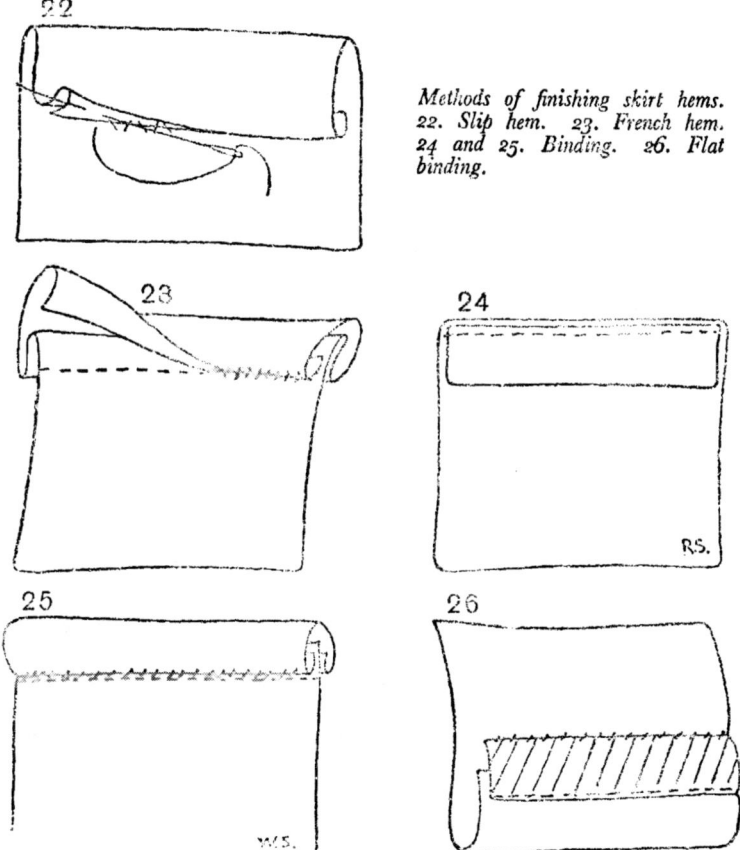

Methods of finishing skirt hems.
22. Slip hem. 23. French hem.
24 and 25. Binding. 26. Flat binding.

Mark A and B. Fold the point over by A and B and crease mark firmly.

Fold A over to touch B with right sides together and machine-stitch by the crease mark, stopping ¼-inch from the edges. Cut the point off from C to B leaving ⅛-inch to ¼-inch turning. Separate the edges of the turning and press flat. Turn the point out to right side and make the hem.

SIMPLE DRESSMAKING

Finishing to Lower Edge of a Blouse

No blouse keeps neatly arranged at the waist unless it is pulled in with elastic.

Make a ¾-inch wide hem at the lower edge. Form a caser by machine-stitching ⅛-inch from the bottom edge of the hem so as to take in ½-inch wide elastic to draw in the fulness. It is wise to make the elastic removable, and for this reason it is worth while using a good quality as one elastic will serve several blouses. The washing, drying and ironing of a blouse becomes much more easily done when the elastic is removed. Work two buttonhole slots one on each side of the side seam. These slots are made on the single of the material on the wrong side of the hem. Sew a button to the middle of the hem so that it comes between the two slots. Make a loop at each end of the elastic which has been cut 1 inch less than the waist measurement. Slip the elastic through the hem and fasten the loops over the button. Instead of the loops and a button, a hook sewn to one end of the elastic and an eye to the other may be used.

For a blouse which fastens right down the front the slots must be worked at each end of the front facing, and a button sewn on in front of each slot. Make a loop at each end of the elastic.

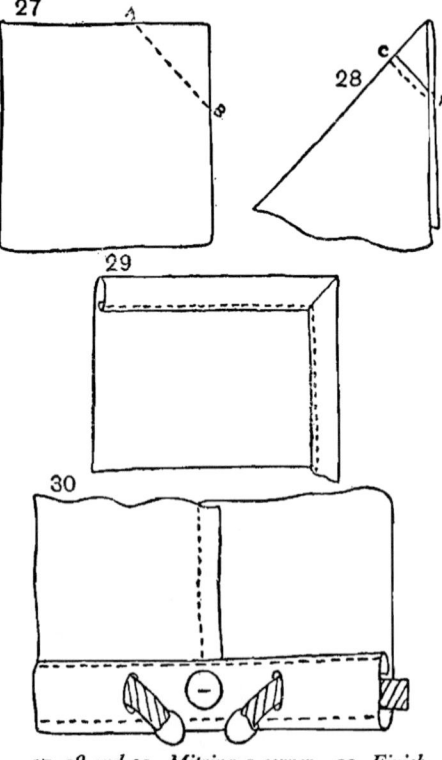

27, 28 and 29. Mitring a corner. 30. Finishing to lower edge of blouse—showing the waist hem with button and loops on end of elastic.

SIMPLE DRESSMAKING

Openings

OPENINGS are made so that the garment may slip easily on and off, and yet give a fitting and neat appearance. These should be constructed to form a decoration, or if hidden should be as inconspicuous as possible. All openings on ladies' garments fasten right over left.

NECK OPENINGS. *Bound.* This method is suitable for cotton and fine woollen fabrics.

Cut the opening down the centre front straight, by a thread. Cut a cross-strip ¾-inch or 1 inch if the material is loosely woven. (Directions for cutting out, see Cutting on the Cross.).

Place the right side of cross-strip to the right side of the opening with edges meeting, taking care to have the end of opening free from pleats. Machine-stitch, or run and back-stitch ¼-inch from the edge, tapering towards the bottom end of opening. An extra stitch or two should be taken here to give extra strength. Press the seam against the strip. Turn in a fold along the edge of strip, then over to touch the stitching. Hem just above the stitching so that stitches do not go through to the right side. Unless this opening has the cross-strip stretched tightly at the bottom end of opening it will not lie nicely.

FACING OR LAPEL OPENING. (For method of working, see chapter on Lingerie.)

SHOULDER OPENING. If the opening is to be on one shoulder only it must be made on the left shoulder. Make before finishing neck-line.

Unpick the shoulder seam for 3 inches to 4 inches. Insert a straight cut strip of lining under the front shoulder seam, tack it by the raw edge and machine-stitch it along to keep the edge firm. This lining is inserted in order to strengthen the edge of opening as the shoulder seam is as a rule on the bias. Flat bind the raw edge and slip hem to garment.

Press the seam of the back shoulder forward. Cut a straight piece of lining the length of seam and 2 inches wide, and place it with right side against right side of back seam. Machine-stitch and turn lining over the edge, and back on to the wrong side. Slip hem the edge down on to the material. This forms the wrap or under part of opening. Fasteners are sewn on or loops and buttons if a decorative finish is desired.

WAIST OPENING FOR A DRESS. When a dress fits closely at the waist it requires an opening and the simplest method is similar to that for a shoulder opening. All openings are placed at the left-hand side and fasten right over left.

The length of the opening varies, but 4 inches below and 4

SIMPLE DRESSMAKING

inches above the waist line gives an average. For the top part, cut a strip of lining 1 inch longer than opening and 1½ inches wide. Insert the strip of lining under the top seam and run-stitch just at the turn over of the seam. Turn seam over by fitting line and machine-stitch by the edge on the right side to keep it firm. Bind the lining and edge of turning together (*Fig. 31*). Wrap or under part. Snip the turning in to the machine-stitching ½-inch above and below the opening. Cut a strip of lining or silk to the length of opening and 2 inches wide. Place right side of lining to right side of wrap and machine-stitch ¼-inch from the edge. Turn lining over the edge and back on to the wrong side and slip hem the turning down on to material. Lay under hem or wrap against the top hem, and loop-stitch the turning at top and bottom down on to the turning of top hem. (*Fig. 32.*) Sew stud fasteners at regular intervals with one at the extreme beginning and end of opening in order to keep it perfectly flat.

31 and 32. Waist opening for a dress. 33. Skirt opening or placket.

SKIRT OPENING OR PLACKET. These do not vary much and the directions which follow will give general rules which can be applied to all skirt plackets.

Placket of Skirt with Raised Seam. The placket should be made

SIMPLE DRESSMAKING

before the turnings of seams are finished. The left side seam is left unstitched from the waist down for about 8 inches to 10 inches.

For top side of placket, cut a strip of lining 9 inches long and 1½ inches wide. Insert the strip under the turning and run stitch to the opening just by the turn over of seam. Turn the seam over by the fitting line and machine-stitch by the edge on the right side, keeping it in a line with the stitching of side seam. Care must be taken to have the stitching neatly joined as there should be no visible sign of connection. Bind the edge of lining and material together with Paris binding. (See directions for Binding Seams.)

For under side or wrap. Cut a piece of material same as skirt 9 inches long and 2 inches wide. Bind one side and one end. Place the wrong side of strip to wrong side of under part of opening, with raw edges meeting, and the bound end of strip 1 inch below the end of opening. Bind the two edges together and carry right down the skirt seam. Stitch across the end of opening to keep the upper and under parts together.

Making and Fixing Collar to Shirt Blouse

IF you have no pattern the following instructions will give you a very good fitting collar.

Take the measurement of the neck from the dress or blouse, and draft on paper as follows :—

    A—B = ½ neck measurement plus 1 inch.
    A—C = 3½ inches.
    E is 1 inch up from D and 1 inch in.
    Curve from A to E, this is the neck line.
    Join E to D.
    F = ½-inch down from C. Curve slightly from F to D.
    A—F = centre-back of collar

To Cut Out. Fold the material so that the selvedge threads run the length of the collar, and place the shape with A=F to the fold. Leave ¼-inch turnings at neck, ends and outer edge. Cut another piece exactly the same and mark the neck curves distinctly.

34. *Marking pattern for collar for shirt blouse.*

To Make Up. Place the right sides of both pieces together and machine-stitch ¼-inch from the edge of outer edge and ends leaving the neck curve open. Care must be taken not to mistake the neck curve for the outer edge. Trim the edges and cut off the points to the machine-stitching, this reduces the bulk. Turn the

SIMPLE DRESSMAKING

collar right side out, poke out the points to take a good shape and tack by the edge of seam.

TO FIX TO NECK. Place the single edge of right side of collar to the inside of neck with centre-back points meeting. Pin and tack the two edges together taking care to have the front edge of opening and end of collar making one continuous line. Machine-stitch ¼-inch from the edge. Press the seam up against the collar. Make a ¼-inch lay on the edge of under part of collar and fold down to touch the machine-stitching. Hem along, taking care not to let the stitches go through to the right side.

In another chapter you will find other and more elaborate collars.

MOUNTING A SKIRT TO A WAISTBAND

WAIST banding or Petersham banding may be bought from 1 inch to 4 inches wide, and may be boned or unboned.

Make the band with large hooks and eyes sewn to the ends on the right side. The right side of the band is next the wearer, and should fasten right over left.

The quickest and simplest method of fixing the band to the skirt is to have the band fastening in the centre-front. Mark the centre-front, centre-back, and side points of both skirt and band.

Place the wrong side of the band to the wrong side of the skirt, with the corresponding points on band and skirt meeting. Keep the skirt ½-inch above the top edge of the band, and pin all round. Insert the pins downwards as in this way they are easier removed when fitting. Fit the skirt and arrange the fulness to lie neatly and regularly all round. Remove the top hook before sewing. Tack with upright stitches, then back-stitch on to the band. Use a strong needle and thread for this process. The ½-inch turning at the top of the skirt is turned over the edge of band and rough hemmed down. The part of skirt from the centre-front to the placket is turned down in a line with the top of band. Finish the raw edges by flat binding with Paris binding or a strip of lining. Sew on the top hook.

Sometimes a skirt has no banding at the waist and is merely finished with a belt made of the same material as the skirt. Prepare the belt by folding a lay all round. The belt should be 4 inches longer than the skirt waist—this allows 2 inches for the wrap, and 2 inches to form a point on the top end of belt. Have the belt and skirt marked at centre-front, centre-back and side points. Place the belt against the top of skirt with an overlay of ½-inch, and corresponding points on band and skirt meeting. A skirt finished at the waist in this manner has little or no fulness to dispose of, or just sufficient to case into the belt. Machine-stitch skirt and belt together along by the lower edge of belt, continue round the point, and along the upper edge. Bind the inside of the belt with a piece of strong lining, or with Paris binding, if it is wide enough to take in all the raw edges. Make a buttonhole at the point of the belt as it is the most secure fastening for this type of waist finishing.

Sleeves

The fickleness of fashion changes the silhouette of the sleeve in a moment's notice, from the plain tailored to the fluffy, frilly, and puffy, on to the massive leg-o'-mutton. We have, of course, the shirt-blouse sleeve which is always with us and varies very slightly with the fashion. Here are a few directions to guide you over the difficulties of making cuffs and setting in your sleeves.

SLEEVE OPENINGS. *First Method.* A narrow hem. This is a very quick method and is suitable for fine woollen or cotton materials.

Make a mark 3 inches from the sleeve seam on the under side then make a $\frac{1}{8}$-inch hem $1\frac{1}{2}$ inches long, running towards the seam. Snip the turnings at the beginning and end of the hem. Gather round the wrist ready to apply cuff.

Second Method. Continuous opening.

Make a mark 3 inches from the sleeve seam on the under side and cut the opening 3 inches long straight up by a thread. Cut a strip of material 7 inches long and 2 inches wide. Now follow the directions given in Lingerie article.

Tack the top part of opening to lie back on the wrong side of sleeve. The under part projects and forms the wrap. For a link cuff, tack both pieces back on to the edge of sleeve at the wrist. Gather round the wrist ready to apply cuff.

Third Method. Fold over. If the sleeve is wide enough to pull over the hand then no opening is required, and may remain loose at the wrist if desired. If the wearer wishes a tight fit then the width is reduced by making loops and sewing on buttons sufficiently far along to fit firmly to the wrist when the loop is over the button. A row of these made up the back of a cuff, or for 4 inches up the sleeve makes a nice decorative finish. Fasteners may be used instead of loop and buttons, but it gives a plain finish.

FIXING CUFF TO SLEEVE. Make cuff double to width and shape desired. Separate the top edges. Place the right side of cuff with single edge to right side of gathered wrist of sleeve, taking care to have the end of cuff and edge of opening meeting exactly. Regulate the gathers and tack together with small stitches. Turn the cuff down by the tacking stitches and machine-stitch on the right side exactly by the edge. Turn up the under edge of cuff, and hem just below the machine-stitching. Make buttonholes and sew on buttons, or sew on fasteners.

An easy method of fixing a shaped cuff to a very full sleeve Gather the bottom edge of sleeve before the sleeve seam has been sewn up. Turn in a lay along top edge of cuff. Pull up the fulness of the sleeve. Lay the top edge of cuff over the gathered edge of the sleeve, taking care to keep the side edges of cuff and sleeve in one continuous line. Machine-stitch along by the top edge of cuff. Over sew the turnings of sleeve and cuff together.

Fold sleeve over so that the right sides are together and side seams meeting, taking care to have the seam of cuff meeting exactly Machine-stitch and press the seam perfectly flat. Finish the edge of the turnings by top sewing, loop-stitching, or narrow hem. If the cuff is too wide finish as directed in third method of sleeve openings

MAKING UP A TWO-PIECE SLEEVE. The inner seams are tacked together beginning at the armhole. The armhole curves should meet and any difference working out at the wrist.

The sleeve must not twist and in order to prevent this prepare as follows : Lay the under part of the sleeve on the table and then place the back edge of top part over to lie exactly against back edge of under part. Pin the seam down and examine carefully If there is a twist you will detect it immediately. Alter if necessary at the back seam. The front seam is rarely altered. Machine-stitch the seams and press open perfectly flat.

Cut a piece of thin tailors' canvas on the cross 4 inches wide and sufficient to go round the bottom part of sleeve. Place the canvas with the edge to the fitting line of wrist and tack round Turn up the sleeve, turning over the edge of canvas and rough hem. *Fig. 40* shows the canvas round wrist of sleeve and the turning rough hemmed.

If a soft finish is required at the wrist do not put in the canvas just rough hem the wrist turning to the coat sleeve.

OPENING FOR FITTING OR TWO-PIECE SLEEVE. Open up the back seam, or dart for $3\frac{1}{2}$ inches above the wrist. Tack back the seam of the top part of sleeve and bind with a piece of lining or Paris binding. Snip the turning of the seam of under part of sleeve at the top of opening and bind the edge. Turn up a lay round wrist and bind in the same way as top side of opening. Lay the under part of opening or wrap against the seam of top part of opening and buttonhole-stitch across the top end. Sew on fasteners or make loops and sew on buttons.

SETTING IN SLEEVES. The setting in of sleeves is a process in which so many amateurs find great difficulty, but this should not be, if the sleeves have been carefully made. They should slip into position without any trouble and a professional touch will be got instead of that " home made " appearance.

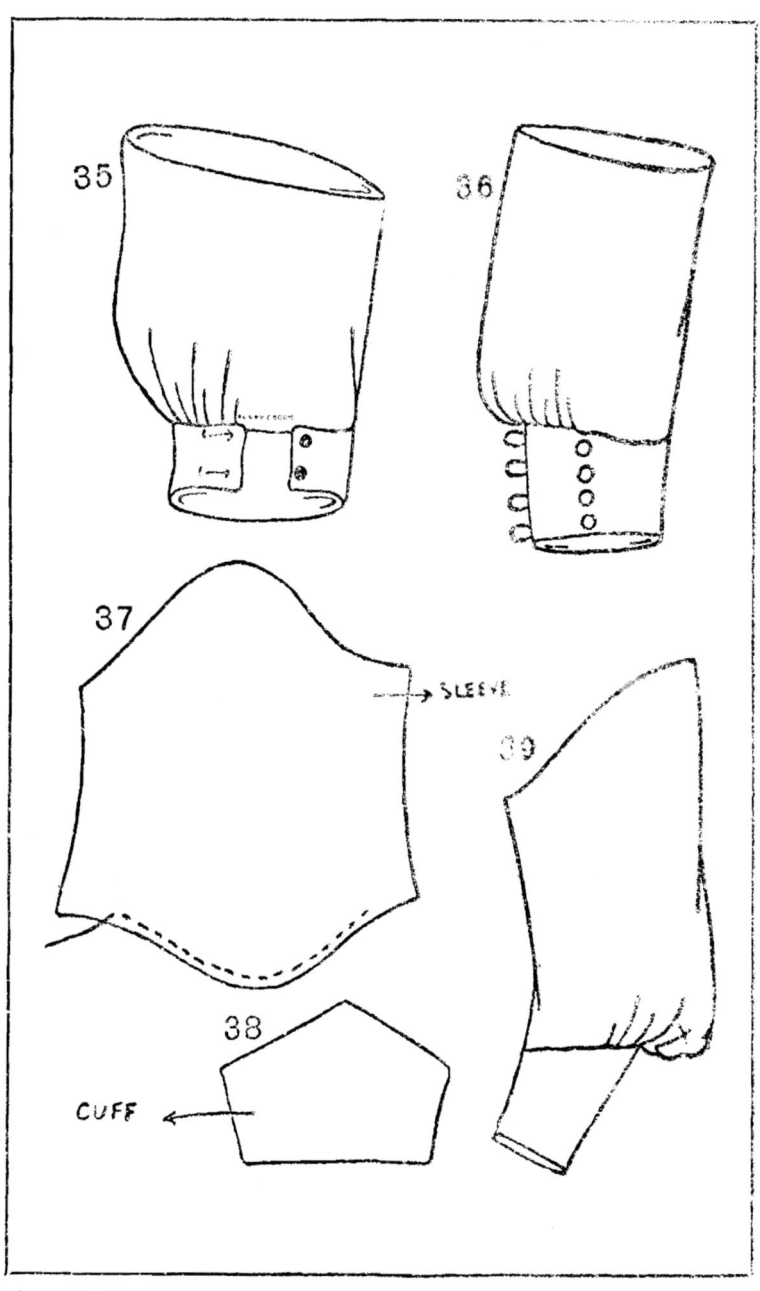

Sleeve openings. 35. First method—a narrow hem. 36. Third method—fold over. 37, 38 and 39. Fixing cuff to sleeve.

SIMPLE DRESSMAKING

COMMON MISTAKES AND THEIR REMEDIES. 1. When making up a sleeve on material which has no decided right and wrong side there is always the danger of making both for one arm, and very often it is not until the setting in comes along that this error is discovered. To avoid this, pin mark the right side of each sleeve before separating them after cutting out.

2. Putting right sleeve into left armhole. This is avoided by placing the sleeves on the table with the seams meeting and the two under parts of sleeve uppermost. Now you have got over your difficulty for the right and left sleeves are lying as they should be when in the garment, the front of the garment facing uppermost.

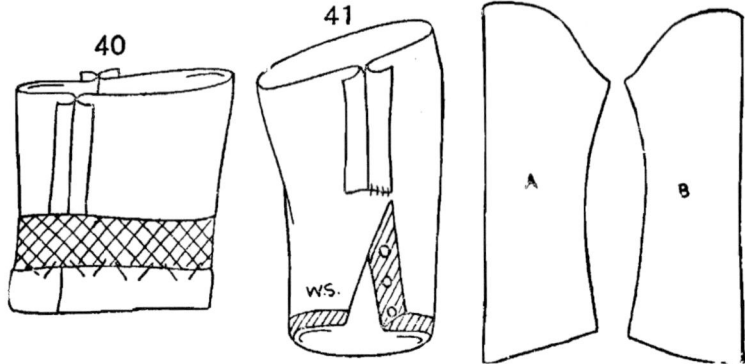

40. Shows the canvas round wrist of sleeve and the turning rough hemmed. 41. Opening for fitting of two-piece sleeve.—A under of left sleeve ; B under of right sleeve.

3. Not having the inset mark—that is the point where the seam of sleeve meets on armhole of garment—clearly marked. This should be done when fitting the garment and if omitted then it must be seen to before setting in the sleeve.

4. Not having the shoulder points marked. Always mark on the sleeve the point which should touch the highest point of armhole, and it should be so placed as to have the straight thread of sleeve running down from this point.

5. Sleeve too tight for armhole. This should never occur. A plain fitting sleeve should always have at least 1-inch more than the armhole measurement of garment. A little fulness is easily disposed of to make the sleeve look perfectly plain. To remedy such a mistake, either let out the seam of sleeve a very little, or take in a very little on the underarm seam of garment. When altering the width of a two-piece sleeve always take in or let out on the back seam.

6. Sleeve too wide for armhole when a plain effect is required. Width must be reduced at the seam of sleeve. The armhole of garment is never reduced unless it itself is at fault.

SIMPLE DRESSMAKING

How to Set In. Fitting of garment and sleeve, see directions given in Fitting. Fold the garment in half and pin the armholes together with shoulder seams and underarm seams meeting. Trim the armholes to ½-inch from fitting line, this will make both exactly the same.

Gather the top of sleeve ½-inch from edge. Turn garment wrong side out, and place the right side of sleeve to right side of garment with the seam of the sleeve to inset mark, or match notches. Pin the under part of sleeve to lie against the armhole of garment about 8 inches in all. Pin from the inside of sleeve, for in this way you have more control over the work. Pull the gathering thread up so that the sleeve fits the top part of armhole exactly. Pin carefully, inserting the pins vertically in order to arrange the fulness more evenly. There should be very little fulness—just sufficient to give a nice roundness to the top of the sleeve without puckers, or pleats shewing, especially when the garment is made of cotton or unshrinkable material. If there should be a little extra fulness when woollen material is used it may be shrunk away with a hot iron and a damp cloth.

Fit the sleeve at this stage and correct any little mistakes. Machine-stitch by tacking thread inserting work into machine with sleeve next needle so as to have control over the fulness of sleeve and to maintain the curve of the armhole. Sometimes sleeves are back-stitched by hand instead of machining.

As a rule the turnings of the armhole are finished in the same manner as the other seams of the garment, but overcasting or loop-stitching gives a nice soft finish. If binding is used let it be of soft cotton or silk. Paris binding is far too hard for this purpose.

French Seam. A quick and strong method for frocks made of any kind of washing material. Never used on woollen, heavy linen of heavy cotton fabrics.

Gather top of sleeve ¼-inch from the edge.

Turn the sleeve wrong side out and place to the wrong side of the garment, with edges meeting, and with the sleeve seam in the correct position. Pin under part of the sleeve ¼-inch from the edge, keeping it perfectly flat. Pin across the top of sleeve by the gathering thread, keeping the fulness evenly regulated. Tack and machine-stitch by the tacking stitches, from the inside of the sleeve. This first row of machine-stitching is on the right side of garment. Trim the raw edges. Pull the sleeve out, turn down by the seam and tack on the wrong side ¼-inch from the edge. Machine-stitch by the tacking. Care must be taken that no raw edges show on the right side of the seam.

The above directions are given for a plain sleeve. For a full gathered, or pleated sleeve the rules are exactly the same, the only difference being that the gathers have to be very carefully regulated. Two rows of gathers help here. If there are pleats then these must be neatly prepared and tacked before setting in.

POCKETS

BOUND POCKET. Have position and size of pocket clearly marked. Tack a strip of linen or lining to wrong side of garment against pocket mark so as to strengthen the work. Cut two pieces of material 2 inches longer than pocket and 3 inches wide.

On right side of garment place one piece to top side of pocket mark, with its edge along by the line to be cut and the other to the under side, having the right sides touching. Machine-stitch along both pieces ¼-inch from the edges, beginning and ending exactly opposite each other and leaving 1 inch free at the ends of each strip. Cut by pocket mark to within ½-inch from each end, and mitre out to the machine-stitching. (*Fig. 42.*)

Press seam open and pull the pieces through to the wrong side. Form a lip on each side of opening taking care to tuck the ends well in. Tack and machine-stitch along the sides and up the ends. (*Fig. 43.*)

Cut two pieces of material to the size of pocket. Place and machine-stitch one piece to top part of pocket binding, and the other to the under part. These two pieces lie on top of each other, and are machine-stitched round to form a pocket. (*Fig. 44.*) If the material used is too thick a piece of lining will do for the under part of pocket.

BOUND POCKET FOR WASHING FROCK. Mark size and position of pocket carefully.

Cut a piece of material 7½ inches long and 1½ inches wider than length of pocket opening. Place right side of this piece to right side of garment, with 4 inches above pocket mark, 3½ inches below and ¾ inches over each end. Machine-stitch ¼-inch along each side of pocket mark, and up the ends. Cut along by pocket mark and mitre to the corners taking care to cut right to the machine-stitching. (*Fig. 45.*)

Trim the edges very slightly. Pull the material through to the wrong side and up over the cut edges, which should meet. Press the turnings at the ends of pocket well back and arrange the fulness into little inverted pleats. (*Fig. 46.*) Tack neatly and from the right side machine-stitch along the sides and up the ends. Turn the top part of material over to lie on the under part and machine-stitch ¼-inch from the edge all round to form a pocket. Turn the raw edges in against each other and top sew.

This method cannot be used on thick woollen materials but is excellent for cotton, linen, silk or artificial silk.

SIMPLE DRESSMAKING

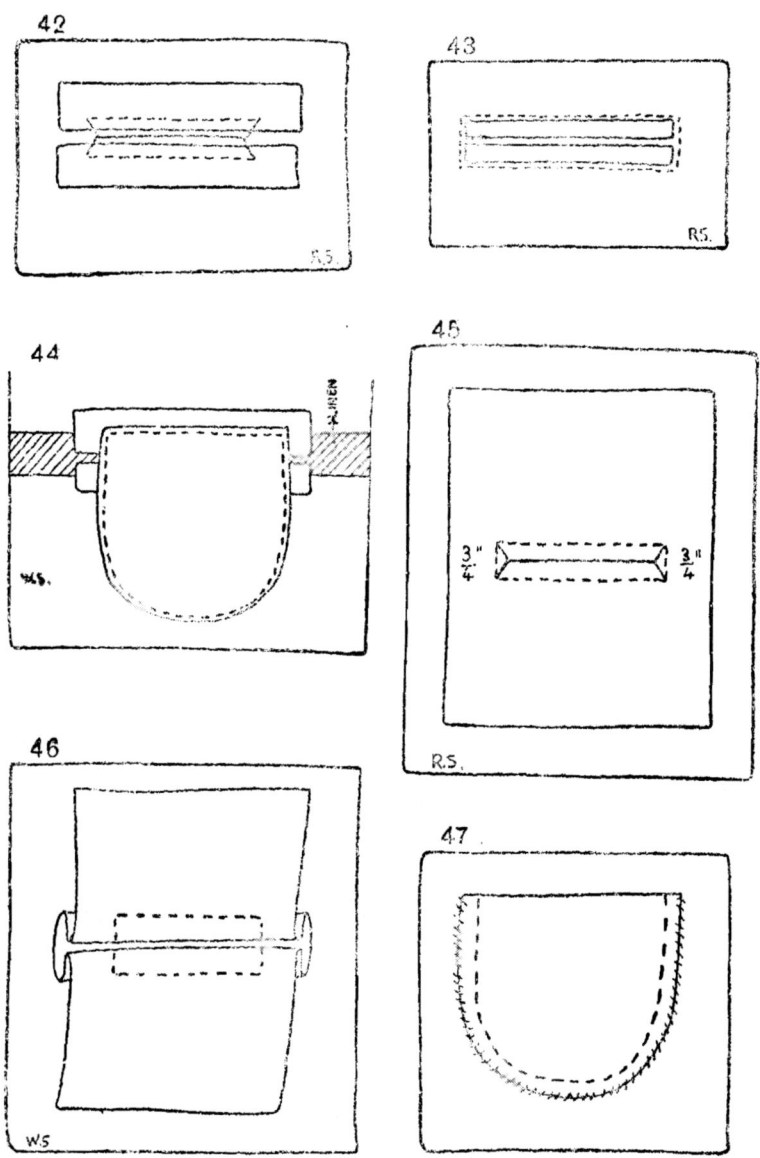

Pockets. 42, 43 and 44. Bound pocket. 45, 46 and 47. Bound pocket for washing frock.

SIMPLE DRESSMAKING

FLAP POCKET. To make the flap cut a piece of material 4 inches long and 5½ inches wide, taking care to match the stripes, or checks of material at pocket mark. Fold in two lengthwise and stitch up the ends. Turn out to right side and tack. Press perfectly flat, and machine-stitch round the edge.

This pocket is now worked in exactly the same method as for Bound Pocket. Use the flap as the top piece and keep it to the right side.

VEST OR STRAP Pocket. Prepare as for Bound Pocket if woollen material is used. Cottons and firmly woven materials do not require a strengthening. To make strap, cut a piece of material 6½ inches long by 5½ inches wide. Turn down 1½ inches and sew up each end leaving ¼-inch free at the raw edge. Turn right side out, snick turning at the edge and press perfectly flat. Place the short piece with the raw edge lying exactly along the under side of pocket mark with right sides together. For the top side cut a piece of material 4½ inches long by 5½ inches wide, and place to top side of pocket mark right sides meeting. Machine-stitch both pieces ¼-inch from the edge. Cut by pocket mark and mitre the corners. Pull pieces through to wrong side and tack strap into position. Machine-stitch along by seam of strap on right side. Make pocket by machine-stitching together the piece of material on top side, and piece which comes from the strap. Machine-stitch the sides of strap to garment.

PATCH POCKET. Prepare as for other pockets if woollen material is used. Cotton and closely woven materials do not require a strengthening. Cut a piece of material to the size of pocket with turnings. Also a piece of lining exactly the same size. Finish the top edge of pocket with a hem to wrong side, or a facing to right side. Place right side of lining to right side of pocket and machine-stitch the sides and bottom edge. Turn out to right side, and tack by the edge, keeping the lining hidden. Hem the lining across the top edge and press. Place pocket into position and machine-stitch to garment exactly by the edge. If the material is a close-woven woollen or a cotton then the lining is not required, but for loosely woven materials the lining strengthens and keeps the pocket in good shape.

RENEWING TROUSERS POCKETS. Remove the worn pockets from the trousers. A strong material such as heavy drill or a firm, closely-woven linen is necessary for trousers pockets. ¼-yard will be sufficient for boys' pockets and ⅜-yard for men's.

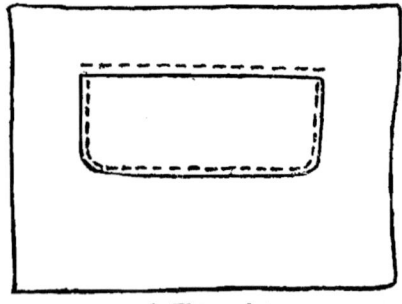

48. *Flap pocket.*

SIMPLE DRESSMAKING

Fold over 5 inches. Measure down from top at cut ends 4 inches, this makes the pocket opening. From there straight in 1 inch and curve round to the folded edge. The slope of 1 inch at the top is to make the pocket slant inwards.

To Make Up. Stitch with a French seam the curved part from the 1 inch round the curve to the fold.

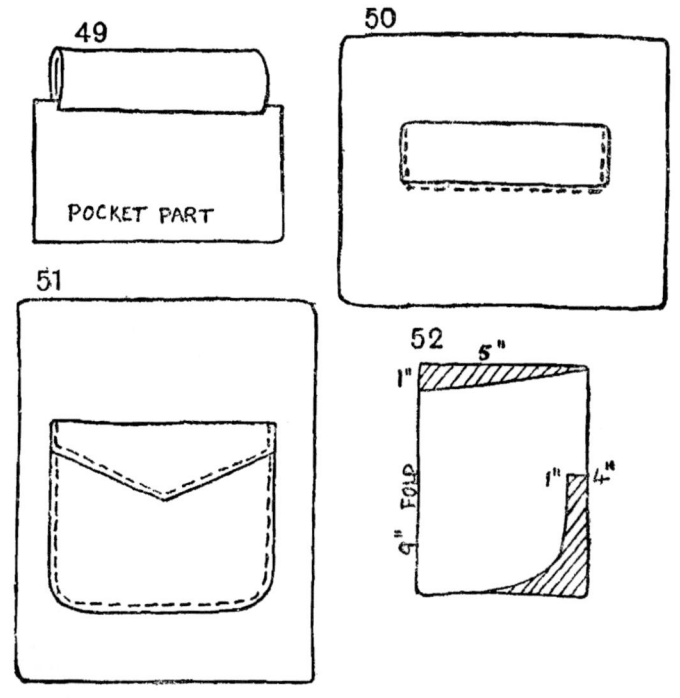

49. *Vest or strap pocket—strap and pocket part prepared.* 50. *Vest or strap pocket.* 51. *Patch pocket.* 52. *Pocket shape for boy's trousers.*

Inserting. The top edge of pocket should run in a line with the edge of the waist, and is caught in with the facing of trouser waist. Turn in the edges of pocket opening and place about ½-inch in from the trouser opening. Hem very firmly with stitches taken through the pocket facing.

Belts

Belts for woollen, cotton, and linen garments are made of double material. Cut strip of material selvedge way 5 inches longer than required and twice the width required, plus turnings for seams. Fold the strip in two lengthwise with right sides meeting,

SIMPLE DRESSMAKING

and machine-stitch ¼-inch from the edge. Press the seam open, and pull through to right side. To do this insert a safety pin through one edge of end of belt. Turn the head of safety pin inside the belt and pull through. (*Fig. 53.*)

Tack seam to lie down centre-back of belt. Finish end by making a point. An easy method of making point is to fold end of belt in two with right sides together and stitch across the end (*Fig. 54*). Trim edges and cut corner off. Open the seam and turn the point out, then hem across the fold. (*Fig. 55.*) This method of pointing can only be used when the material is fine and closely woven.

Another method of making a belt is to cut material as directed above. Fold the strip in two lengthwise with right sides meeting and machine-stitch ¼-inch from the edge also stitch the shape of point (*Fig. 56.*)

Cut the turnings from the point and turn right side out. A ruler is very good for this purpose. Begin at the point and pull the belt over the ruler until it appears at the open end. Tack into position with the seam coming along the edge, taking care to poke the point well out to make a good line. Sew buckle on to other end. Sometimes a fastener is sewn on to the point to keep it perfectly flat when belt is being worn.

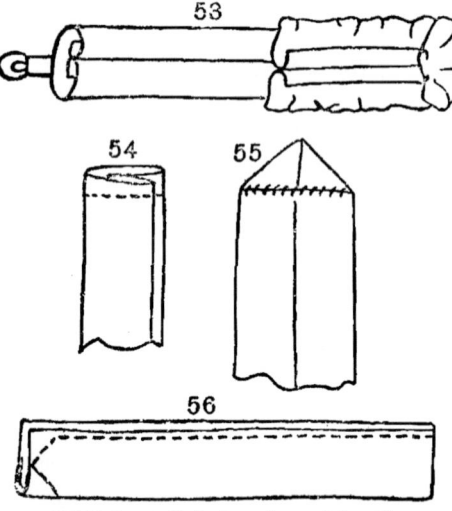

53. *Belt being pulled through to right side.* 54. *Making point of belt.* 55. *Finished point of belt.* 56. *Another method of making a belt.*

BELT SUITABLE FOR SILK MATERIALS. Take a piece of petersham ribbon the colour of frock, and the width of belt required. Point one end of the ribbon. Cut the material sufficiently wide to cover both sides of the ribbon plus turnings for seams. Place the ribbon to the middle of wrong side of material. Turn one edge of material over the edge of ribbon and bring the other edge over to meet. Make a turning and hem along centre-back. Take care to make the pointed end perfectly neat. Sew buckle on to the other end.

If the material is transparent make the foundation of belt of stiff muslin, and cover in the same way as directed above.

SIMPLE DRESSMAKING

BELT SUPPORTS. Belt supports are required at the side seams in order to hold the belt in position. These are made of the dress material about ¼-inch wide. Cut a strip of material 1 inch longer than width of belt and ⅜-inch wide. Fold over and hem down on the wrong side. Make a turning at the top and bottom of tab and sew firmly to the side seams in the position required for belt.

Another method is to make a thread loop. Take a strong thread and make three strands then across these make loop stitches close together. The making of loops is fully described in the Needlework Section. This is less bulky than the other method and is excellent for washing frocks.

FASTENINGS

1. Buttons and Buttonholes.
2. Hooks and Eyes.
3. Hooks and loops.
4. Loops and buttons.
5. Press Studs or Dome Fasteners.

BUTTONHOLES. The directions for working buttonholes are given in Plain Needlework. When working on cotton, artificial silk or linen fabrics use cotton or mercerised thread. On woollen fabrics a silk twist is used and the buttonhole-stitch is worked all the way round to give special strength to the end.

BOUND BUTTONHOLES. Mark the position of the buttonhole. Cut a strip of material selvedge way 1½ inches longer than buttonhole and 2 inches wide. Place the centre of strip to buttonhole mark with right sides meeting. Machine-stitch ⅛-inch along both sides of the buttonhole mark and across the ends. Cut through the two thicknesses of material by the buttonhole mark, and then snip diagonally up to the ends of the stitching. (*Fig. 57.*) Pull the strip through to the wrong side, press it out perfectly flat, and tack round the slit. On thick material let the strip show on both sides, forming a lip.

If the garment is unlined turn in the raw edges of strip and slip hem to garment. (*Fig. 58.*) If there is a facing, merely tack into position at the back. Place facing over the top, and cut a slit exactly opposite the buttonhole. Turn in an edge and hem to wrong side of buttonhole. (*Fig. 59.*) This method is also used when making slots for pulling through a band.

BUTTONS. Mark the position of button. Make a back-stitch exactly where the button is to be sewn.

For a four-holed button form two bars, which should run in the same direction as buttonholes.

Leave a stem between garment and button. Wind the thread

SIMPLE DRESSMAKING

round the stem tightly then take the thread through to wrong side of garment and finish off thread.

LINK BUTTONS. These are used for shirt blouse sleeve links. Take two buttons, and use a strong cotton or silk twist thread. Connect the two buttons together with strands of thread keeping them ½-inch apart. (Fig. 60) Buttonhole or loop-stitch across the strands and finish off the threads.

HOOKS AND EYES. Hooks and eyes are made of twisted wire and can be bought in black or white. Use a strong cotton thread or silk twist and buttonhole or blanket-stitch round the rings. The shank of the hook is sewn down at the turn-over to hold it down firmly.

PRESS STUDS OR DOME FASTENERS. Fasteners are made of metal and can be bought in black or white. Use a strong cotton thread or silk twist. Blanket or buttonhole-stitch three times into each hole. On passing from one hole to the other put the needle in beside the last stitch and slip the needle through the next hole. Never have a long stitch showing from one hole to the other.

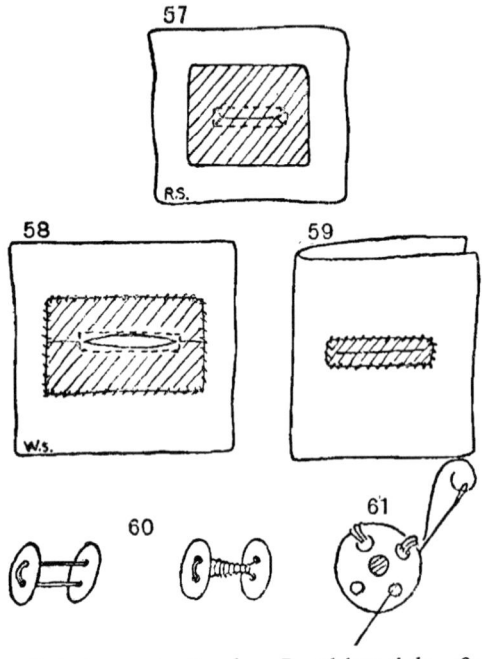

Fastenings. 57, 58 and 59. Bound buttonholes. 60. Link buttons. 61. Press studs or dome fasteners.

Sew the flat side of a fastener to top side of opening.

Loops and eyelets are fully described in the Needlework chapter which opens this chapter.

ARROW HEADS

ARROW heads are used as a decorative strengthening. They neaten such awkward corners as the ends of darts and pockets. The two methods described are worked on a triangle.

Begin by marking the shape to any size desired with chalk or tacking threads, or may be cut in cardboard which will guide in marking in chalk or pencil.

SIMPLE DRESSMAKING

Bring up the needle from the back of material at point A. Insert needle in at apex B and bring it out on the base close to the last stitch. Insert the needle again on the centre line just under the last stitch taken at B. Continue in this manner working in the section A B D.

Repeat as directed above, filling in section B C D, taking care to have the stitches meeting at the centre line.

Fig. 62 shows how to begin work on the arrow. *Fig. 63* shows the arrow when it is finished.

Second Method. Bring up needle from the back of material at point A, then lift two threads at apex B. (*Fig. 64.*) Insert the needle at C and bring it out close to the stitch at A. (*Fig. 65.*) Insert the needle on the triangle just under the stitch at apex B and bring it out on the triangle at other side of stitch at apex B. (*Fig. 66.*) Continue in this manner until the whole is filled in. *Fig. 67* shows the finished appearance of the arrow head.

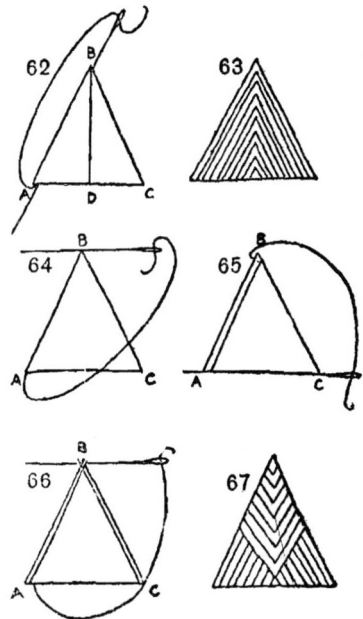

Arrowheads. 62. How to begin the arrow. 63. Finished arrow. 64, 65, 66 and 67. Second method of making arrowheads.

Order of Making Up a Simple Coat

CUTTING OUT. Instructions for this will be given with your pattern and should be carefully followed.

Mark the waist-line, centre-front, and pockets if any.

PUTTING TOGETHER. Tack pieces together and fit. Pay particular attention to the neck and shoulders lying perfectly flat. Mark the armhole curves, the fronts, and set of lapel.

Machine-stitch the darts on the shoulder, cut open and press perfectly flat.

Machine-stitch the side seams and press thoroughly. If the facings are cut on to the coat, turn them back on to the wrong side of garment and tack into position. Rough hem the raw edges of facing down on to coat.

If the facings are cut separately, place the right side of the facing to the right side of the coat easing slightly at the lapel, especially at the corners. Machine-stitch and press the seam open flat. Turn over by the seam, keeping the facing slightly beyond the edge of coat. Tack into position and rough hem the raw edge of facing down on to the coat.

If a stiff front is required, canvas must be put in between the coat and the facing. Few coats have this unless they are made of a heavy or loosely woven material. (*See* Method of Fixing Canvas to a Coat.)

Make pockets if required. (*See* Pockets.)

Make up sleeves. (*See* Making up of Two-piece Sleeve.)

LINING COAT. The lining of a coat should be eased into the garment so that it will not cause puckering in the coat.

68. Showing lining tacked into coat.

Always have a small pleat down the centre-back of lining, and a pleat on each front shoulder. The lining stops in front at the edge of facing.

It is much easier to fix in a lining to a coat before the shoulder seams are machined up. By doing this you can get your garment to lie flat on the table.

Tack, machine-stitch, and press open the side seams of the lining. Place the side seam of lining to the side seam of the coat with raw edges meeting, and run-stitch together. Do likewise with the other seam. Lay the pleat down the centre-back of the coat and baste down almost to the foot of coat. Baste the lining and coat together across the back and round the armholes. Make the pleats on the shoulders and baste down. Take care not to go too near

SIMPLE DRESSMAKING

shoulder when basting—give yourself enough space to stitch and press the seam on the coat material. Baste the lining over the edge of the front facings.

Join the shoulder seams of coat and press perfectly flat.

Lay front shoulder lining forward on to the seam, and bring the back shoulder lining over. Turn in an edge and hem across.

Level the foot of the coat, and rough hem along by the raw edge of turn up. The lining may be turned in and hemmed ¼ inch above the bottom edge of the coat. Another method is to leave the lining free at the bottom edge, and if so, finish the lining with a narrow machine-stitched hem.

Slip hem the lining to the facing down the fronts.

The sleeves are lined by placing the wrong side of the lining to the wrong side of the sleeve with front seams meeting. Take care to place together lining and sleeve for corresponding arms. Run-stitch the two seams together. Turn the lining out over the sleeve and tack together about 4 inches down from armhole. Hem the lining round the wrist about 1 inch above the turn up of sleeve. Turn the sleeve right side out. Set in sleeves. (See directions How to Set In.)

Press round top of sleeve. (See directions for Pressing.)

The lining of sleeve is now brought up and hemmed to the machine-stitching of sleeve.

FIXING CANVAS TO FRONTS OF A COAT. Have fronts and set of lapel fitted and marked. Shrink the canvas thoroughly.

The canvas is cut on the bias to fit the fronts of the coat with 1½ inches over the shoulder and clearing the bust line.

Place the front edge of canvas ⅛-inch from the fitting line of coat and tack so that it lies perfectly flat. Keep the lapel almost free from tacking stitches. Tack from the right side in one direction only—from neck to bottom edge.

Mark with tacking stitches the break of lapel through the canvas. Pin a strip of linen ¾-inch wide weft way down the break of the lapel slightly straining the linen.

Pad-stitch the lapel beginning at the break and working to the outer edge. To pad-stitch insert the needle from right towards left in a horizontal direction and lift a small stitch about ⅛-inch.

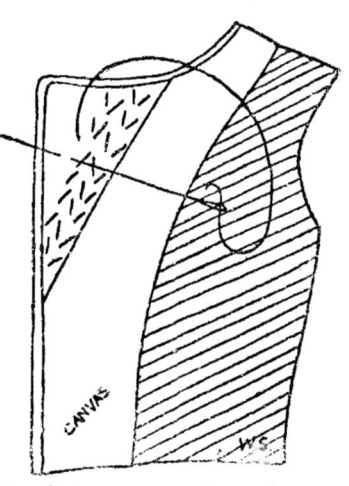

69. *Fixing canvas to fronts of a coat.*

SIMPLE DRESSMAKING

Go forward $\frac{1}{2}$-inch and repeat in this manner right up to the top. Do not turn the work, but work the same stitch coming downwards. The stitch is really a tiny basting stitch and the two rows of stitches appear in a V-shape. *Fig. 69* shows the lapel being pad-stitched.

Trim the front edge of canvas to be $\frac{1}{4}$-inch from the front fitting line of the coat. Tack a 1-inch strip of linen down the edge

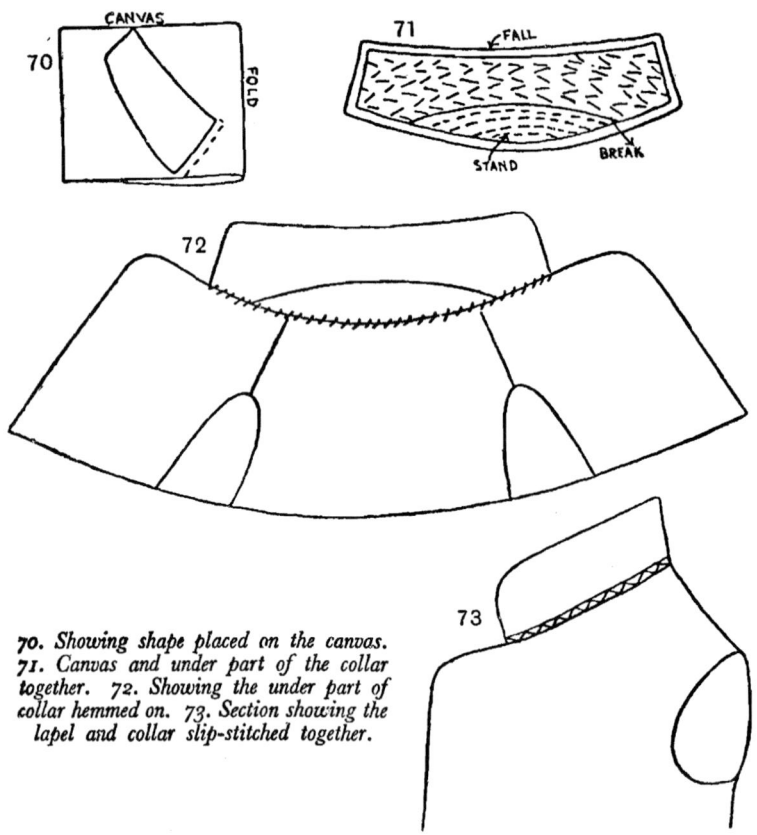

70. Showing shape placed on the canvas. 71. Canvas and under part of the collar together. 72. Showing the under part of collar hemmed on. 73. Section showing the lapel and collar slip-stitched together.

of fronts and rough hem to the canvas. By doing this you avoid machine-stitching the canvas in with the fronts, and facing and so reducing the bulk, also it softens the edge.

Tack the facings to the fronts with right sides together. Ease the facing to the lapel in length and width, especially at the corners. Keep from waist to bottom edge perfectly flat. Machine-stitch exactly by the fitting line. Trim the edges and turn out to the right side. Tack down exactly by the edge, and again 1 inch from the edge. Turn the lapel back into position and tack over the break.

A COAT COLLAR. *Interlining.* Place pattern with the centre-back to the cross of the canvas. Cut by the pattern lines, but leave ¼-inch at the centre-back for a join. Join up the seam, and fit. Mark the break, that is the turn over at the neck.

Under part. Cut the under part of the collar from the material exactly the same as for the canvas, but allow ¼-inch turnings all round.

Machine-stitch up the centre-back and press perfectly flat. Place the seam of the interlining against the seam of the under part and tack the two together. Run and back-stitch by the break line. Machine-stitch the "stand" in rows of ⅛-inch apart and pad-stitch the "fall." Rough hem the neck turning of under part to the canvas. Fold over by the break line and press into shape.

Top part. Cut this part in one piece weft way and ¼-inch turnings all round.

Stretch the neck edge and the outer edge of the collar shape. Place the right side of upper part to the material side of the under part, easing the top to the under especially at the corners. Machine-stitch together along the back and up the ends. Trim the edges and cut the points off the corners. Turn the collar right side out and tack into position exactly by the edge.

FIXING TO COAT. The under part of the collar is placed to the coat first.

Pin the centre-back of under collar to the centre-back of the coat. Tack into position taking care to have the ends of the collar meeting the fitting marks on the lapel, and that both sides are exactly the same. Hem to the neck line of the coat, using a strong thread and keeping the stitches close together.

Turn in the edge of upper collar, and tack so that the edge just touches the edge of the lapel. Slip-stitch these edges together. Press firmly.